Undeniable
Faith

How God Kept Me

by
Shelly Clanton

Copyright ©2022 Shelly Clanton

Brenda's Editorial Service

All rights reserved. No part of this publication may be reproduced, distributed, or transmitted in any form or by any means, including photocopying, recording, or other electronic or mechanical methods, without the prior written permission of the publisher, except in the case of brief quotations embodied in critical reviews and certain other noncommercial uses permitted by copyright law.

All Scriptures are taken from the King James Version of the Holy Bible. The King James Bible is in the Public Domain.

ISBN: 978-1-951300-42-5

Liberation's Publishing – West Point - Mississippi

Dedicated to

This book is dedicated with love to my handsome brother, Dion, who passed away in June of 2020.

His last words to me were, **"Sis, finish your book!"** His memory will be forever embedded in my heart.

Our Hands

Undeniable Faith

Contents

Chapter 1 7

Chapter 2 13

Chapter 3 17

Chapter 4 23

Chapter 5 27

Chapter 6 33

Chapter 7 39

Chapter 8 47

Chapter 9 53

Chapter 10 59

Chapter 11 63

Chapter 12 69

Chapter 13 75

Chapter 14 81

Chapter 15 85

Chapter 16 91

Chapter 17 97

Chapter 18 103

Chapter 19 109

Chapter 20 115

About The Author 119

Chapter 1

Shelly Clanton is my name. I am a proud mom of two gorgeous daughters and four precious grandbabies. With God's grace and faith, I raise my daughters to be respectful and humble women; it was particularly challenging, but I tried the best way that I know how too. They were my number one priority: caring for my girls. I tried my best to keep them active in school, occupy their minds with sports, books instead of other activities that they could have easily gotten into. At the time, I was taking my girls to volleyball practice, basketball games, and girl scout meetings to keep them busy. I loved my daughters so I wanted the best for them so they would grow up to be independent and owning their own business. While the girls were in school, I was home alone which gave me so much time to think about life and where I wanted to be in life.

Many days had passed, and I wanted to call my former therapist to talk with her about life issues that I thought would not bother me anymore if I did not think about it or talk about it. That is a lie! My internal medicine doctor suggested that I see a therapist because of some past issues about which I have never talked about. I now agree that talking to a therapist was a great idea because it helped me the most. I have learned that in life we all have demons or have been in a dark place and have fought extremely hard to push through. I have been in that dark place for a long time where I felt like I was alone, I felt like no one cared and I also felt like I should run away because I did not matter to anyone.

Back in the seventy's, my parents were trying to keep food on the table so we may have been left at home alone with a sibling, uncle, or grandparent. Most days, we were left at home because our parents were trying to survive and put food on the table. The person we were left home with was not caring at all; this person only cared about themselves, and they turned out to be a monster. That person loved to walk around naked or sit around fondling themselves in front of me. Yes, a family member! Knowing what I know now, I do believe that God will take care of his children. This sick act went on for years. When I got the courage to talk to my mom and her siblings about what was happening, the family pushed it aside like it did not matter. Truth be told, this is child molestation, and it should have been taken seriously. My God is an awesome God, and I will tell this story. Why? Because it needs to be told.

If you are being molested by a family member, friend, or anyone, please tell someone. It is not your fault that this person is a sick human being and need psychological help, please tell someone. You are a child of God, and no one should do this to you. As a little girl, I am thinking that something was wrong with me. You are not the sick person here they are. Years passed and the molestation stopped but the memories are still there. Being molested by a family member is a terrible and sickening behavior that many of us have endured throughout our lifetime but with the help of a therapist and your faith in God, you can feel some closure, happiness, or relief. Keep in mind that you cannot do this alone, seek help. Keeping your appointments with your therapist and your faith in God, you can conquer anything. It is hard, it is not easy; it can be done.

To move forward in life, I needed to process the pain, which was a struggle, but I was willing to put in the work for someone that is willing to listen. Put in the work to set yourself free because you never know who may be watching you. If you want to move forward, you must have faith in God to help you go through the process to make a change. You will most likely have to step out on faith or step out of your comfort zone to make a change and do not be afraid you can do it. I can honestly say that my faith in God has taken me an exceptionally long way. If it had not been for God on my side, I do not know where I would be right now. I had to realize that God is greater than any storm. To have faith means having a strong belief in God or in the doctrine of religion.

Lying in bed at night, I would find many verses or passages to read in the Bible about faith. I also love to read my Bible daily. One was, in *Mark 11:22, "And Jesus answering saith unto them, have faith in God." In John 3:16, "For God so loved the world that he gave his only begotten Son, that whosoever believeth on him should not perish but have everlasting life.*

Growing up and I listening to my friends talk about how they couldn't accomplish anything or wanted to go to school to pursue their career, but something was stopping them from pursuing their career. Most of them say that it has a lot to do with their past or how a single parent raised them. Our community meaning (blacks) do not like to seek counseling to help with our issues in life and I think that this is a problem. We should not have a problem seeking help from a licensed mental health counselor or therapist. Many years have passed, and I prayed to God about what I experienced in life. I have sought professional help and I have begun to heal. Living life and raising two daughters was a struggle for me but by the grace of the God He allowed me to raise two beautiful, intelligent, and smart women.

As the years passed, I began to pay attention to my past relationships, I realized that keeping a male companion was difficult for me. At that moment, I did not know why or why we were at this breaking point in the relationship, it fell on me. Being in a committed relationship, it did not last long because I had trust issues. Looking back over my past; thinking about everything I went through, I realize that God has brought me an exceptionally long way from being molested, abused, and misunderstood. My God still gave me the strength to live life and take it one day at a time.

Chapter 2

There were days that I could barely get out of bed or if I got out of bed, I was too tired to move from the bed to the couch then back to the bed. I started to experience breathing problems, swelling in my joints and hair loss. From going back and forth to the internal medicine doctor, I learned that I have this pulmonary disease called sarcoidosis. For about three years my ankle and joints would swell up a lot, but I blew it off because I was going a lot with the girls to different activities or practice, and I could not afford to miss practice or a game. I was thinking the pain and swelling came from me running around on my feet a lot. After three years had passed, I noticed one day my ankles turned a dark purple and at that time I decided to go to a rheumatologist. It took me two months to see a rheumatologist. Then I was diagnosed with arthritis.

The rheumatologist gave me medication for swelling and something for the pain. We were going back and forth to a rheumatologist for years until one day I noticed on my right arm that I had a purple rash. The rash itch so bad from that day forward I began to pay close attention to it for a year. About every three months, the rash would appear again on my arm for two to three weeks then disappear for a while and come back. I decided to go to my internal medicine doctor to see if he could give me some creme or something for this rash and tell me why I was having shortness of breath a lot. My breathing was not like it should be. After going to my internal medicine doctor, I had to have a biopsy of the rash which was on my arm. The biopsy was taken, and I had to wait a couple of weeks for the result. After going to the doctor for the results, it came back with sarcoidosis! Talking to myself at the time, I said sarcoidosis.

What is that? I asked my doctor I have never heard of that, what is it? My doctor gave me a pamphlet with little information on it and I went home and my later that afternoon my mind began to rumble wondering what sarcoidosis is, where did it come from, how did I get it, can my kids get it, so many different thoughts going through my head. I do not know. After that day at the doctor's office, I promised myself to do my own research about sarcoidosis. I cannot forget about my daughters. I was taking care of them and praying that my health would not fail so I could keep going for them. My daughters were my motivation.

As the years passed, I began aching a lot in my joints and sometimes I had a little shortness of breath but that did not bother me because I was still going. What really slowed me down was when my heart rate would skip a beat, or my heart rate would beat extremely fast. I could feel it through my clothes which scared me sometimes because I was wondering what is wrong? My internal medicine doctor suggested that I make an appointment to see a cardiologist (heart specialist) We went to my cardiologist appointment, and she decided that she wanted me to wear a heart monitor for two weeks. Really? Okay whatever the doctor suggested so we can find out why my heart rate is beating over 160. I wore the monitor for two weeks and went back to the doctor to be told that I have pulmonary hypertension.

What pulmonary hypertension? Geesh!

So, this is another thing that I must add to my list to do my own research on too, pulmonary hypertension, sarcoidosis, and arthritis. From my experience, I have learned that the doctors will tell you what you ask or know little about what is going on with you. It is up to you to do your own research and it is up to you to take care of your body. I do not think that you can learn all there is to know about an illness or a disease because I am still learning about sarcoidosis and its side effects.

Let us talk about pulmonary hypertension. Pulmonary hypertension is a type of high blood pressure that affects the arteries in the lungs and in the right side of the heart. In some people, pulmonary hypertension slowly gets worse and can be life-threatening. There is no cure for some types of pulmonary hypertension. Treatment can help reduce symptoms and improve your quality of life. Pulmonary hypertension symptoms are fatigue, dizziness, chest pains, shortness of breath (dyspnea), and a racing heart or heart palpitations.

Chapter 3

Sarcoidosis is a lung disease that can affect any organ in your body but your lungs and lymph glands. Abnormal masses or nodules called granulomas consisting of inflamed tissues forms in certain organs of the body in which they may alter the normal structure of the organs. There are many symptoms, one is shortness of breath, coughing, fatigue, hoarse voice which is something that happens to me often swollen joints, red and teary eyes, or blurred vision, dry skin, wheezing and muscle spasms just to name a few. In some cases, sarcoidosis can cause hypercalcemia?

Sarcoidosis can raise blood levels of vitamin D, which stimulates your digestive tract to absorb more calcium. Hypercalcemia causes an increase of calcium in your blood because of calcium receptors in your body. Sarcoidosis can cause diabetes or long-term use of prednisone that can cause diabetes. Sarcoidosis can affect the pancreas and may contribute to diabetes. Relying on corticosteroids for the treatment of sarcoidosis should be minimized in those who have diabetes. I have been on prednisone off and on for 25 years and now the doctor says that I have diabetes as well, so I must watch what I eat and drink.

I do know that God is a miracle worker, and my healing is coming soon. If it had not been for God on my side, where would I be? I have had many days where I did not want to get out of bed, but I have two reasons to get out of bed, my girls. While I was sitting at the girls' volleyball game, I felt this quick sharp pain in my chest. Twenty minutes later, I felt this pain again. I will be going to the heart specialist in a week, and I will let her explain why I am having these pains. After another appointment with the heart specialist, my doctor told me that these sharp chest pains may be coming from inflammation in the chest wall pertaining to sarcoidosis.

The cardiologist suggested that I should carry around with me this little pill to put under my tongue if I have another chest pain. The next day, I had another severe sharp chest pain! The pain hurt my chest so bad after it went away my chest was sore for a couple of days, and I was tired. Those chest pains did not feel good at all, and I had them often. I was told by the cardiologist that if I have three or four pains, I should go to the emergency room because it may be something else like a heart attack. For ten to twelve years, I used nitroglycerin for years two or three times a week for my severe chest pain and most of the time the little white pill helped. After a while, the severe sharp chest pain stopped. Before my daughters graduated and left home, they witnessed me being in pain a lot and I tried extremely hard for them not to see me in so much pain, but I could not help it.

My daughters are my world, so I kept them busy. Senior year was coming up for my oldest. What an awesome time to get to see your daughter walk across that stage to receive their diploma. Shareka graduated from high school and went on to college in Atlanta, Georgia to become a Mental Health Counselor. Being a loving mom, I am proud of my babies. Yes, they are in their thirty's, and they are still my babies. Shannon graduated from high school and went to college in Atlanta, Georgia and has her degree in Fashion Merchandise. Time does not stop; life goes on. When my babies move out to go to college, I had a lot of time on my hands. My family was still in Mississippi, so I decided to stay around for a while. As the years passed by, I went from going to the doctors once a month to going to five different doctors twice a month. I kept my Bible close so I could reach for it and read my favorite scripture which is *2 Corinthians 5:7; "For we walk by faith, not by sight".*

A lot of my time was spent at home because I did not want to have those terrible chest pains which felt like a muscle spasm. One morning, I woke up to a terrible stomach pain. My stomach was hurting so bad I was crying. Months went by and I never went to the doctor to find out why I had such terrible stomach pains. This one night before bed, I had this severe pain in my stomach. This time I had to go to a gastroenterologist because the pain was unbearable. So now I am wondering what is going on with my body. As I waited three months to see the gastroenterologist (stomach specialist), I was becoming increasingly angry with myself because of the pain. My stomach would hurt severely if I drank milk, ate ice cream or anything sweet. I would feel bloated, had heartburn, trouble swallowing, diarrhea and abnormal bowel movement. The time had come for me to go to the gastroenterologist and to tell you the truth I could not wait any longer. We went through three or four tests which included a CT scan and a colonoscopy. Doing the CT scan, I had to drink this thick, white milky substance for the scan the day before. These tests produce images of your abdomen and pelvis that might allow your doctor to rule out other causes of your symptoms, especially if you have abdominal pain. Your doctor might fill your large intestine with a liquid (barium) to make any problems more visible on X-ray.

When that day came for me to have the colonoscopy done, I relied on God because I was extremely scared; everything went well. The results came back; I did not have cancer spots or swelling anywhere. The results being IBS. So, I am thinking to myself what IBS is. IBS is a disorder that affects the large intestine. The symptoms are exactly what I was experiencing: cramping, abdominal pain, bloating, gas, diarrhea and/or constipation. What is next?

The doctor prescribed medication to help manage this, another medication added to the list. Oh well, there goes more medication added to my already lengthy list.

This medication is called Dicyclomine (Bentyl), Pregabalin (Lyrica), or gabapentin (Neurontin) which they might ease severe pain or bloating. I am thinking to myself this is too much! For a while, I began to feel normal meaning less pain and not being so tired. I also noticed that my feet did not swell as often.

Chapter 4

I started to feel pain and redness in both of my eyes. The right eye would hurt a lot and sometimes I would see something like a tiny blinking light or something floating in my right eye. I made an appointment to go to an ophthalmologist to make sure my eyes were doing fine. After four or five appointments to the eye doctor, I was told that I have glaucoma and it is affecting my right eye severely. The pain and the floaters are what the doctor called it. I needed to have laser surgery to release pressure from my right eye before I lose my eyesight. At the eye doctor, we did the eye exam and the visual field test which determine the severity of my eyes. I found out that certain medications can cause eye damage as well. I constantly must remind myself that all medications have side effects.

The internal medicine doctor always encouraged me to get my eyes checked regularly because of the Plaquenil medication I was taking for my skin rash. Plaquenil is used to treat lupus erythematosus and rheumatoid arthritis. My internal medicine doctor had me taking it for the skin rashes and I know that it helped a lot. The rash does not break out on my arm and stomach as often. The rash would usually appear at least once every two months. It would itch bad for two to three weeks then disappear. After using Plaquenil, the rash would appear once every four or five months; it would stay at least a week then disappear. So, I decided to go to the eye specialist to check my eyes and thank God that I did.

What is glaucoma? It is a condition of increased pressure within the eyeball, causing the loss of sight. The pressure in my right eye was extremely high every office visit. In my right eye, I would feel pain in that eye, blurred vision, pain, and redness most of the time. Sometimes, I would see flashing tiny lights in my right eye. After the first visit with the eye specialist, I sat in my car and cried, and I asked God what should I do? God answered and said rely on me! Right away, I stopped crying. I realized that God heard me all I needed to do was to have a tiny bit of faith in Him and I will be fine.

We made an appointment for the laser surgery and continued taking the medication until the surgery date.

Laser surgery was performed which is partial removal of the eye's drainage system to help release pressure from the eye. I thought that it was going to be painful and complicated, but it was not. We were not in the office long and it was an outpatient procedure. After the laser surgery, I went home, rested for a few days and was back to my old routine and as of this day, my right eye is still doing very well. Thank God!

That is when I decided to visit my daughters who live in Georgia. I was so happy that I could still visit my daughters whenever I wanted to. From time to time, I would experience a little pain, or my breathing gave me a problem, but it was nothing that I could not bear. I decided to continue to live my life one day at a time. A friend and I decided to meet one another for lunch and throughout the day I was experiencing side pain. Because of the pain, I decided to tell my friend about the pain I was experiencing. She recommended that I go to the ER because at the time I was not using the restroom. That was a Friday when I met her for lunch and that Sunday, I was in the emergency room with severe stomach pain. The stomach pain turned out to be gallstones. Yes, something that I had never heard of.

What are gallstones? Gallstones are hardened deposits of digestive fluid that can form in your gallbladder. Gallstones range in size from as small as a grain of sand to as large as a golf ball. Some people develop just one gallstone. There were many gallstones in my gallbladder which tore my gallbladder and I had to get it removed by laparoscopic cholecystectomy. I kept the faith throughout this journey, and I made sure that I continue to read my Bible and go to bible study and church on Sunday. My Faith in God is what kept me going day after, day after, day after day.

Chapter 5

You know sometimes believing and trusting in something that you have never seen before can be a tad bit discouraging. But what other choice did I have? I needed something or someone. I started going to an eye specialist every month because my right eye was damaged more than my left eye. From that day forward, I started using eyedrops in my eyes every day and at night. Life was great but something was missing. It is time for me to get my life back on the right track. Yes, my daughters were with me every step of the way, but they had their own lives, and I was not going to be a burden to them. My faith in God was my motto. Since I was visiting my daughters often, NaShay asked, "You should move here with us?" I asked her to give me time to think about it because I was traveling back and forth a lot so moving would be ideal! Why not move? Okay before the big move I sat down and talked with my mom and my aunt, who was battling cancer. I had to assure my aunt that if she ever needed me, I was a phone call away and I had no problems coming back home to help her.

In preparation for the move, I was tired, I was always hot, heart palpitations and wheezing a lot so I made a doctor appointment with the pulmonary doctor to find out if I had fluid on my lungs. The doctor admitted me to the hospital that day. I had to put the move on hold until I got better. The doctor orders a CT scan which is when you use a computer and a rotating x-ray machine to scan your body. It can show soft tissues, blood vessels, heart, and bones in various parts of your body. The CT showed that I had fluid on my lungs. Later that afternoon, the doctor came back to my room to inform me about the procedure that she was going to do in the morning which was to insert a tube in my chest to drain fluid.

The morning came, I was prepared for the procedure, and it went well. I was awake when she numbed the area on the right side of my chest and inserted the tube. I felt pressure but that was it and the tube was inserted in the upper right side of my chest. After four days, the tube was removed, I watched the doctor gently pull the tube from my chest and I was thankful for the doctor because she was caring and patient. Thank God for guiding the doctors and nurses and for giving them the wisdom and the knowledge to perform their jobs. I always try to take great care of myself so eating right and exercising is important. One second, you are smiling enjoying life and the next second, you are on the floor in excruciating pain that is coming from your chest. Why does it happen like that? I do not know why, and many doctors do not know either. Every chance I get, I read about sarcoidosis and the many effects that it would have on a person's life. Everyone would not be treated the same.

You can learn a lot by doing your own research and studying about your illness.

On this day, I was doing my regular sit ups and one or two push-ups, and I immediately saw a picture of my aunt with a worried look on her face. I felt this sense of loneliness and confusion. As I lay on the floor contemplating on whether I should call my aunt or not, I became worried. I gathered myself and called my aunt to check on her. She begins telling me that she is doing well but sometimes she does not have a ride to her appointments. My emotions took over. I asked my aunt would you like for me to come home to make sure that you have a ride to your appointments, she asked me, "would you do that for me?" My response would be would you like me too? She said yes and I asked her to give me two weeks to get myself together and I will be home. About two weeks later, I moved back home to help my aunt and my mom.

My aunt, Lasie, was my best friend. We could talk about everything. I hate that she was battling breast cancer, such a horrible disease. Most of the time, I hated to take her to chemo treatments because the treatments were harsh on her body. There were many nights I laid awake praying and hoping God would heal her body. One Saturday afternoon, my aunt was not feeling well, and we had to take her to the emergency room because she was in a great deal of pain. They admitted my aunt. Days went by and I needed to take a drive, so I drove to the Sonic drive thru. On my way back home, this quick flash of my aunt lying in a casket paralyzed me. The cheese sticks and the ranch flew into the windshield; I pulled over at the store to gather myself. As I lean forward, I laid on the steering wheel and cried my heart out! That image did not make me feel well at all. I felt terrible! After crying and praying, I gathered myself and pulled off heading back home. I did not tell anyone about that vision because I did not want it to come true but a week later, my beautiful aunt passed from cancer. We did get a chance to talk before she departed from earth. We had a lengthy conversation, and I must admit I knew her last thoughts. I am glad we had that conversation; it was something that she wanted to talk to me about for a while. Three months later, I began to think about that image of her in that casket and now, she is no longer here, it is painful. Before the passing of my aunt, I would have dreams that really did not make sense to me.

Death is an event that we will never get used to, but it will always be a part of life. There have been many days and nights where I would have visions or a dream that I could not explain; what was happening or why it was happening. A week after my aunt's death, I was admitted in the hospital for severe chest pains. I was told by the doctor that I had pneumonia which was not anything new to me. I suffer from pneumonia often because of sarcoidosis. I stayed in the hospital for three days hooked up to an IV bag and antibiotics.

While in the hospital I made sure that I read *Philippians 4:5-7* which states, "*Let your moderation be known unto all men. The Lord is at hand. Be careful for nothing; but in everything by prayer and supplication with thanksgiving let your requests be made known unto God. And the peace of God, which passeth all understanding, shall keep your hearts and your minds through Christ Jesus.* I was not understanding the reason for such sickness and turmoil that was going on in my life, so the Bible was my safe haven. Most of the time when I read the Bible and waited a while that pain or feeling was gone.

Chapter 6

I began to feel at home in Georgia finding my way around and meeting new people. I was living with my daughter and working a part time job which was great. Days and months passed then years passed. By me working with the public, I met people, and everything was fine at the time. I would drive to Mississippi every month to see my family. When I was living in Mississippi, the weather was different than the weather in Georgia. If this makes any sense to you at all, the Mississippi heat felt like dry intense heat compared to Georgia's heat, hot and humid.

At the time, I was having dinner dates with my daughters on the weekend and loving life all at the same time. There were many days I thought of my aunt and what she went through, how I felt about her sickness and why she went through many things made me sad. She was a comedian, a loving, caring and a beautiful person. The last conversation we had I will always cherish for the rest of my life. She was a true soldier in the army for God and I will love her until eternity. Most of the time reading the Bible helped me to overcome pain, confusion, sadness, and depression. In the book of *Job 15:20*, it reads *"The wicked man travaileth with pain all his days, and the number of years is hidden the oppressor."* And for that reason, I began reading the Bible more. It was such a happy go getter for me and a comforter. I would read a passage and it would make so much sense to me I would write it down on paper and meditate on it. This is another verse that kept me feeling like I mattered. In the book of *1 Corinthians 14:33*; *"For is not the author of confusion, but of peace, as in all churches of the saints."*

 I thought about attending college to receive my degree in Biblical Studies and to learn more about God, his disciples, faith and so much more. By reading the Bible, it kept me focused on what I needed at that time in my life because most of the time I felt depressed, and I had so much on my mind that I wanted to do. Here I am a young lady dealing with a lung disease and I have never smoked a cigarette or cigar a day in my life. I have been around people that have smoked but I did not smoke. Staying focus and trying not to fall into a depressive state kept me going. I would open the Bible to the book of *1 Peter 5:6; "Humble yourselves therefore under the mighty hand of God, that he may exalt you in due time."* I made a promise to myself that I was going to stay in church and continue to seek after God's heart. The more I attended church the more I wanted to know about God. What an awesome feeling! The deeper I got into the Bible the more I wanted to know about Him.

Every day I ask God for forgiveness because I knew there was something that I was doing that God was not satisfied with. The more I read the Bible, the more I wanted to be like Him. The Bible was getting interesting, and I wanted to know more. On Wednesday nights, I would attend bible study and on a Friday night, I would attend church service and on a Sunday morning, I would attend Sunday service. This was done on a regular for two to three years.

One Wednesday night, I met a nice gentleman. The conversation went well for some months then we decided to go to the movies together. We went to the movies together and everything was going so well I began to panic. It has been years since I have been on a date and enjoyed myself, so this was like new to me. I felt like I should call this off until a later date. We went to my favorite restaurant, which is Red Lobster, and we enjoyed the meal, a movie then we went home. I continued to see this young man and the relationship developed into something lovely and worth trying it. The times that we spent together were lovely. We would talk about family, friends, and overall life in general. There are times we would make plans to go out to catch a movie and when the time came, I could not go because of migraine headache or pain in my legs, joints, or fatigue. One evening I invited my friend (Peter) over to watch a movie and talk with him about my health. Before the relationship gets serious, I wanted to make sure that he knew what was going on with me and my life. Well, he came over and the night went well. We discussed his life, his job, and we discussed my life and my health, and I was happy that we had that conversation because it did not change anything. Peter remained the same handsome, loving, and caring person he was when I met first met him. I wanted to make sure that he knew about the migraines, fatigue, Remicade treatments I was taking every 6 weeks, prednisone medication that I was taking that sometimes made me gain weight, the problems that I have with my eyesight, just about everything that is going on with my health. He stated it did not change his love for me.

What a feeling! I finally met someone that cares for me and not for what we can do for each other. As life went on this day, Peter came home early. As he walked in the door, he was moving his right arm around in a circular motion like it was hurting. I asked him "What's wrong?" He stated that he thinks that he strained a muscle in his arm. Every time that he moved his arm, it hurt. Every time that he moved it backward, he felt pain. Every time he moved his arms forward, there was major pain. He made an appointment to see a doctor. After going to four to five doctor appointments, he found out that he tore a rotator cuff in his arm. A rotator cuff are tendons and muscles that is located near the joint in the shoulder. Peter needed surgery on his rotator cuff to repair it and it took up to 6 weeks to heal. To heal meaning going to rehab for a couple of hours a day so he could not work. He made his mind up to have the surgery and it was a success, thank God. For six weeks, he was home with me recuperating and taking physical therapy. We would go to church, Bible study, revivals, spending that quality time together and when his shoulder was better, he went back to work.

Chapter 7

One night around 2am, I was sleeping but I had a terrible dream that woke me up. I jumped up staring at the wall, I left out of the room and went into the living area. I began to pray, why? Because that dream scared the daylight out of me. The dream was about my four nephews who were in a car accident; the car was totaled, and no one survived the accident. Wow! The dream felt so real! I prayed, I prayed, and I prayed because I did not want this dream to come true. I met this young lady at church, and she became my prayer partner. I called her to explain to me about the dream and the both of us began to pray again. I was crushed because in this dream I saw my nephews face very clearly. The next day after eating breakfast, I called my nephews one by one to see what they were doing and were they alright. I did not tell them about the dream that I had the night before. I did not tell anyone about that dream but my prayer partner. I really did not want to think about that dream again.

Two weeks went by while we were home watching

TV, I received a phone call from my mom telling me that my nephews were in a terrible car accident, my heart skipped a couple beats. She said they are all fine. I had to sit back in the chair and breathe for a second because I thought the worst. Thank God, the guys are fine, God was watching over them because it could have been worse. The next day I spoke to my prayer partner, and I was telling her about the accident that my nephews were in, and that the car was a total loss, but the guys came out of the accident unharmed without a scratch. My prayer partner would always say if you had a dream or if something stays on your mind for a period, get down on your knees and pray about it. That is what I began to do; pray about my dreams or visions. I think of that as a miracle worker. God was watching over my nephews right on time. We are grateful to still be able to thank God for another chance at life with my nephews.

From that night forward, I began to take my dreams and visions that I was having seriously. God is a miracle worker if He does it for anyone else, He will do it for you. All you need to do is have faith, keep believing it is going to happen, and the patience to wait until it happens. It is all on God's timing not ours. He will answer when it is time. After that dream, I had no doubt that God answers prayers. I know what God was saying to me, but I did not want to respond. I did not think that I was ready for God calling. God was saying to me come to work for me to help build his kingdom and I want you to go out into the world to tell others how great and awesome I am. I was not ready to be the chosen one for God.

After six weeks, Peter went back to work. While he was off work, there were times when we were in a financial strain with bills and the vehicles, but life must go on. As time passed, I was getting tired a lot, coughing, and getting headaches three times a day. My ankles would hurt more often than normal, and my breathing was not normal. I was short of breath a lot more and I could barely do anything as far as going to the grocery store or walking in the mall with the grandbabies, something was happening, I was noticing a change in my health. I decided to make an appointment to go to the doctor to make sure everything was alright. With Sarcoidosis, if the weather changes, your body will make a change. The appointment was two weeks away, so I made sure that I did not overdo it by babysitting or going out to places with friends. Before I got ready to go to my appointment, I read *John 3:16* which reads, *"For God so loved the world, that he gave his only begotten Son that whosoever believeth on him should not perish but have eternal life."*

I made sure that I downloaded the Bible app to my phone. I could not go without reading scriptures every day. I will never forget this day. It was on a Friday afternoon around 1:30 in the month of May. I went to the pulmonary doctor office to make sure I did not have pneumonia or the flu. Dr. Seed came into the office and explained to me that he wanted me to do a six-minute walk. I stated to him that I may not be able to because I was having migraines and they were bad. The medical assistant came into the office to begin the six-minute walk. I walk for a total of 30 seconds, and I leaned against the wall. The medical assistant asked me if I needed to sit down, and I said yes! As I was walking back to the room, and as I laid on the table my heart rate was beating at 170ish per minute, my oxygen was dropping, the next thing I heard was she needs to be admitted in the hospital, I said what? I was admitted to the hospital for a racing heart rate, my oxygen level was extremely low and my migraines headaches.

What a time I had in the hospital the doctors could not figure out why my heart rate was beating so fast, nor know why I was having migraines. I was given morphine for the pain, and it helped but I could not keep shooting up morphine. This episode had me in the hospital for a total of 13 days. My mom and family came to Georgia to help my daughters so someone would stay at the hospital every night with me. My body was tired. I had aches and pain in the joints. I was wheezing more even after using my nebulizer with the albuterol medication in it. It was a sarcoidosis flare up and it was a bad one. I had a rash on my stomach two weeks ago, but I did not pay that much attention until that fifth day in the hospital. The rash was getting dry and itchy, and it was slowly going away.

The first day in the hospital, I had the IV and

antibiotic dripping through my veins. I could not get rid of the migraine headaches. When I would sit up my headaches would hurt terribly, but when I laid down it went away. I tried it again, I sat up for 5 minutes, my head started to hurt bad, then I laid down and it stopped.

The doctor noticed my pain. The neurosurgeon looked concerned; he had a reason too. I was concerned as well. An hour later, the doctor and a nurse came into my room to explain what he thought was going on with these headaches. The neurosurgeon could not tell me a reason as to why, but he thinks that he has a solution. The solution for the terrible migraines was called an epidural blood patch, something I have never heard of before in my life. The doctor stated he was sure that it would help the headaches. The way that the blood patch works is you draw blood from a vein on my hand and insert the blood in the tiny hole through my back. In other words, plug the leak/hole with the fresh blood. It only took about five to six minutes, and the procedure was finished. The area of skin on my back was numb. I felt a pinch, but it did not hurt at all. To do the procedure, I was lying on my back, praying, of course.

I asked God to guide the doctors' hand and please give them wisdom and knowledge. I was praying hard and long on this one because the thought of inserting a tiny hole in my back was nerve wrecking. I do not like epidurals.

Chapter 8

After an hour, I was able to sit up without having a headache. I was grateful and blessed! I stayed in the hospital eleven days and my back side was getting tired. I was doing so much better; my heart rate was back to normal, and the migraine headaches were gone, and I was ready to go home. I thanked the medical staff for caring for me and the next day, I went home.

Most of the time when you have a flare up, give yourself two days or a week and you are fine, but this flare-up lasted too long, and it was scary. My friend and I had a long conversation about how far we wanted to take the relationship because I am not willing to stay with a man and not get married. I tried it before, and it did not work for me. So, we decided that we would try it for a while to see how we like it. Everything was back to normal. I babysat my grand baby for a few days and if I wasn't babysitting, I was probable at the hospital. I decided not to wait another two months. I made an appointment for the next week. The reason I made that appointment was because I was having chest pains often like once a day. To describe the pain, it was like a muscle spasm in my chest. Most of the time, I would have two to three rounds of spasms a day. If I ever got to four, The doctor suggested to go to the emergency room, and that is what I did. I was going often like once a week. The pain in my chest was excruciating and I would always call on the Lord, why?

Nothing else helped. I was putting nitroglycerin, a small white pill, under my tongue for a preventative measure. Sometimes, you would think that I am having a heart attack. Lord, I thank you! If it had not been for you on my side, Lord, where would I be? I sat down and talked to my partner about the appointment, and I was telling him about my concerns, but he knew what to say God's got you, do not worry. The next day, I went to the pulmonary appointment, and I had to do the PFT test which is a pulmonary function test first. It is a test to measure how well the lungs are working. The gauges measure how the lungs are expanding and contracting (when a person inhales and exhales) and measure the efficiency of the exchange of oxygen and carbon dioxide between the blood and the air within the lungs. The test only takes about 15 minutes but when you are finished you are tired and coughing your head off.

The next test that needs to be done is the six-minute walk. Remember, I tried that test two months ago but failed. I am going to do it this time and pass the test. The nurse came to my room with her timer to ask if I was ready. I said, "Yes! Let us do this!" I walked around the corner heading straight down the hallway before I could get halfway down the hallway, I fell slightly on the wall gasping for air. I thought about a scripture, *Galatians 5:25, "If we live in the Spirit, let us also walk in the Spirit."* The nurse asked me," do you want to sit down?" I said no let us try this again, three seconds later, I was back on the wall. The nurse helped me into the room, and I laid on the table again. I was breathing like I was running a marathon and I was winning; I am thinking to myself; something is not right. The doctor and the nurse came back into the room. I was laying on the table trying to catch my breath and the doctor say to me, "Ms. Clanton, you need to be on oxygen 24/7." I said, "what?" The doctor stated that my blood oxygen levels was below 50.

I asked if that was bad, and she said, "yes!" The

doctor was naming some of the symptoms of low oxygen and I am saying to myself, Lord, yes, I do get that way, Lord yes, Lord thank you, again. The doctor mentioned headaches, shortness of breath, confusion, and chest pain just to name a few; I was experiencing all of them. I sat up to talk to the doctor and she explained to me that this is serious and that I need to take care of myself. After a long visit to the doctors, I made it home and the oxygen tanks made it five minutes before I did. Whew! Oxygen tanks! What a life! I have not had enough time to explain this to anyone, I felt so small and worthless, yes, Lord, I did. The doctor stated that I need to be on oxygen 24/7 and to sleep on it as well. WOW! I cannot do this, I kept thinking that to myself. I cannot do this!

After talking to my daughters, family, and friends, I did not have a choice. If I wanted to live, I needed to wear this oxygen tank 24/7. That night I do remember staying up late watching TV and reading the Bible, the Psalm of David. In *Psalms 23*; *"The Lord is my shepherd; I shall not want. He maketh me to lie down in green pastures: He leadeth me beside the still waters.*

He restoreth my soul: He leadeth me in the paths of righteousness for his name's sake. Yea, though I walk through the valley of the shadow of death, I will fear no evil: for thou art with me; thy rod and thy staff, they comfort me. Thou preparest a table before me in the presence of my enemies: thou hast anointed my head with oil; my cup runneth over. Surely goodness and mercy shall follow me all the days of my life; and I will dwell in the house of the Lord forever." I pray day and night. It does not matter where I am at home or in the car. I would always hear a voice say to me, "Amen." I never in my life thought that it was strange. I just pay close attention to when it happens.

Chapter 9

My life changed now. I must walk around in Walmart, subways, and the malls wearing an oxygen tank. Can I do this? I had time to prepare myself for the public. The tanks were brought to me around Tuesday or Wednesday and church service was on Sunday. Reading the Bible to me was my peace of mind. When I felt discouraged, depressed, hurt by family, lonely, defeated, or tired there were so many Bible verses that I could read that picked me up. When I felt lonely at times, it was painful. Loneliness can lead to depression and frustration. Loneliness to me is a lack of appreciation and that feeling is the worst. The Bible verse that I would read for loneliness would be *Isaiah 41:10, "Fear thou not; for I am with thee; be not dismayed, for I am thy God: I will strengthen thee; yea, I will help thee; yea, I will uphold thee with the right hand of righteousness."*

Oftentimes, I felt discouraged because every move that I made I needed to wear the oxygen. I was worried about what people would say or how people would look at me when they saw me with this oxygen tank. Taking out the necessary time to study and meditate with my Bible, I read a sentence or two that I will never forget. It stated God will keep you. He will meet you in the middle of your discouragement and not let your feet be moved. At that moment, I smiled, and I cried, why? I realized that God was holding me because I was so weak, I realized that without this Bible, I am a nobody and I also realized that I am a child of God.

The loneliness did not end there. I have had many days of loneliness but after so many repeated feelings of loneliness I thought to myself God has other plans for my life hold on beautiful, you are closer than you think. How many of you know that depression is real? I was in a dark place, and I did not care about no one or anything. I did not care if my hair was combed or not, who cares? In *Deuteronomy 31:8, "And the Lord, he it is that doth go before thee; he will be with thee, he will not fail thee, neither forsake thee: fear not, neither be dismayed.* Depression affects how you think, feel, live, sleep, eat, and your daily activities and so much more.

There were many nights where I only slept four or five hours. I would forget a lot and I did not want to do anything at all. The headaches I was having at the time were terrible. Can you imagine having 7 or 8 migraine headaches a day to where the headaches would have your eyes red and the only medication that would stop these headaches for two hours were a BC powder or a Tylenol? After about an hour and a half, another headache would come. I was miserable! Out of all these issues and problem, I have never thought about suicide in which that is a major part of depression. I have never had any suicidal thoughts or any suicide attempts.

As I prepared for church Sunday morning, I had a talk with my partner and said to him that I will explain to the church what is going on with me; meaning let everyone know why I need to wear this oxygen tank. He stated if that is what you want to do, I am behind you. That Sunday before church, I prepared a 15-minute speech. I walked into the church carrying the oxygen tank. As I sat in church watching everyone come in and hug each other, I began to stare slightly to my right, and noticed a mother of the church wearing an oxygen tank as well. You never heard her complain and she always came to church pushing her oxygen on a cart. I will never forget her beautiful smile she kept on her face. Before church service was over, the pastor called me to the front. As I stood before the congregation, I had everyone's attention. I go on to tell everyone about Sarcoidosis and how it has affected my breathing and how I must be on oxygen 24/7. I go on to say that the doctor says it is what I need to survive. As I began to close out my 15-minute speech, one of the mothers of the church that always comes to church dressed beautifully in white raised her hand. As she walked slowly toward me, she stated to me I have Sarcoidosis too. My eyes were wide open, and my heart started to beat fast.

As she spoke into the mic, she said it has been 25 years for me and the doctor says there is no cure for this, but I am fine with this because He still finds time to wake me up and He lifts my spirit and soul, and He will do the same for you. I said, yes ma'am. As she was talking the usher of the church came up to me and held me and said, thank you. I am looking like (what did I do) she stated I have never known so many people that have Sarcoidosis and I have it too. Lord, I begin to cry!

Listen to me! I prayed to God to be with me as I express how I am feeling and why I am feeling this way. I leave the church feeling like a million dollars. Why? Because I am not alone, there were three people in my church struggling with the same illness. The following Sunday, I went to church looking like a million dollars with an oxygen tank on my side.

From that day forward, me and Ms. Day were the best of friends. I helped her to purchase a lighter oxygen tank, the one that you can carry on your side. Sad to say, she passed away a year later from complications from Sarcoidosis. I loved her dearly. She never came to church without that oxygen tank and that million-dollar smile. She made me realize that determination can get you through anything.

From that day forward, I was determined. I am determined to be an advocate for Sarcoidosis until the researchers find a cure; I am determined. One day someone will be diagnosed with Sarcoidosis, and I can hope to be a phone call or an email away. I started going around to different churches to speak about Sarcoidosis and how it affects you and your loved ones. During my pain, I also felt like I needed to do more. As I was sitting at home thinking about what I should do, I decided I should go to college because I really did not have the energy to do anything else. I was living in Marietta, Georgia. The school that I researched was about 45 minutes away, I said, why not? We went to the school, talked to the counselors and the president, and I was pleased with the answers.

Chapter 10

During all this, I began having terrible migraines every day; four or five times a day. My daughter stated, "Mom, please go to the ER." I took her advice and they kept me, that is what I did not want them to do. I was admitted for rapid heart rate, a fever, migraine headaches and an infection. After blood work and x-rays, we prepared for a two or three day stay which ended up being two weeks. The doctors ran many tests, MRIs, and cat scans to determine why I was having terrible migraines that would not stop. I was relaxed but my heart rate was at 105-150 beats per minute. After many appointments with the heart specialist, I was told by the cardiologist that I have pulmonary hypertension.

What is pulmonary hypertension? Pulmonary hypertension is when the blood pressure affects the arteries in your lungs and the right side of your heart. So now I am thinking to myself this is a lot to deal with, then I think about how God is still carrying me. I have never made a clock to wake me in the morning, which was God's work. I still have a chance at life, this is me talking to myself. I still have shortness of breath when I am sitting down watching TV. The fatigue, dizziness, chest pain, and racing heart is a struggle. You know there have been many days that I could not play with my grand baby, but I thanked God for letting me see her/him smile, that is a blessing within itself.

There were many days that I noticed that my lower abdominal was huge, I just ignored it. That is part of the struggle, fluid within your lower stomach. In most cases, pulmonary hypertension is a life-threatening disease, but it can be treatable, and manageable. So, for many years, I have been taking a high dosage of channel blockers to prolong my life. As I laid in bed waiting on answers from doctors, I focus a lot on what God is doing in my life. Also, what courses am I going to study in college and what am I going to do with my degree? Days later, it was determined that I was in a Sarcoidosis flare up which meant I was in terrible pain and aches because Sarcoidosis was taking over my body, and right now, the only medication that will help to control this is Prednisone. I began the Prednisone pack, cortisone shots, antibiotics, and pain medication and within four day I was back at home.

I promised myself I would go to school, get my degree, and take care of myself in the process. That is what I did. I enrolled in Carver Bible College where I met some wonderful students and professors. I was excited about going to college to pursue my degree in Biblical Studies. One of my favorite books I loved to read is "Grasping God's Word by J. Scott Duvall and J. Daniel Hays; awesome books to read that to help explain the process of interpreting the Bible. I am in my room studying and this voice says to me, you can do this, stay focused. I am thinking to myself, yes, I can. Now I am going to college four days a week, studying a lot at night, and loving it but little did I know that my partner was not liking it. We decided to sit down and talk about what he was feeling, and it blew my mind.

With me being on oxygen 24/7, I could not work, and he was the only one working in the home. He wanted out of the relationship; can you imagine how I was feeling at the time? Can you imagine what is going on in my head? Can you imagine? He continues to explain, and I am thinking to myself, really? Right now? The next day, he was gone when I came home from school. Here I am sitting in my home with bills and no money, and I felted lost and depressed! I asked myself what's next? I thought about a short prayer, I asked God to strengthen me through this season of my life, I cannot do this without you, I need you every step of the way, every second of the day, and every minute on the clock, help me! Lord, I am yours and I am depending on you to see me through in your name, Lord. Amen.

To me, life was perfect but in the blink of any eye your life can change. To be in your forty's depressed, disable, and alone could easily take you to an early grave if you let it. My God, I need you now!

Chapter 11

The Lord knew that I did not have many choices because I did not have enough income to stay in my place and pay the bills on my own. I cried for a while, but I did not just focus on that pain because if I would have, I would have still been there. I know what it feels like to be judged because you have a medical illness. For a while, I felt like a nobody. Studying to get my Associate Degree in Biblical Studies helped me tremendously. I was reading my Bible every day and doing so helped me write this essay for college.

I waited until the weekend, and I talked with my daughters about my life. At the time, my youngest had her own place and she had enough room for me. As bad as I did not want to move in with her, I did not have no other choice. My baby offered to help me and asked me to move in with her. What a blessing she is to me. On most days, I was not feeling well so I forced myself to get up and go to school. I did not miss a day of classes. Sometimes, you must do that, give yourself a nudge to continue to push forward.

There were days when I just could not believe what

happened and how could someone be so mean. He really acted like he did not care at all. Some people can be heartless, and that was a heartless move coming from a man that went to church every Sunday and Bible study on Wednesday nights. During that struggle, I became worried and that bothered me because my faith in God was being tested. I also thought about my friend, someone that I could talk with about anything. I was reading at the time and these words were stuck in my head. "Be flexible and reach out to those God has placed in your path."

The next week, I was admitted to the hospital again with pneumonia. I had to stay in the hospital for 5 days hooked to an IV taking different medication and having breathing treatments. God is still good, and it is because of his goodness and mercy that I am still here to talk about it. I asked God over and over to take care of me because I cannot do this by myself.

As I sat in church on this Sunday morning, we were having testimonial service and a young lady, her husband, daughter, and son went to the altar. As the young lady spoke to the crowd about her family's ordeal, my body jerked. When my body jerked, it is like something is within my view and the feeling takes over my body, disturbing my soul. As I listened to the young lady explain about how her family needed prayer, I felt a sense of loneliness, depression, and sadness, but it wasn't for the mother. It was for the little girl who looked about 10 or 11 years old. My heart was hurting because I was feeling sad and depressed for myself. When I got home, I prayed for that family, and I continued to pray for that family. It was a month later in church, someone asked the church to pray for this same family that has stayed on my mind for three weeks, why? The mother found out that the dad was molesting the little girl. I cried so hard that day, why? I felt something that burned a hole in my heart, and it did not feel right at all. God is a way maker and a miracle worker. All He asks of you is a tiny grain of faith and He will take care of the rest. *Hebrews 11:3* states, "*Through faith we understand that the worlds were framed by the word of God, so that things which are seen were not made of things which do appear.*"

This situation brought back memories from two

years ago. I thought about how the Lord had been blessing me repeatedly. I owe it to Him to do the best that I know how to be; obedient to the word of God and to love and care for my brothers and sisters. However, not fully understanding what is going on or why the Lord chose me, I made up in my mind to listen and obey!

This morning was the day that my funds were deposited into my account. I was sitting at the breakfast table drinking orange juice and eating a toast when this smooth, calm voice said to me all your funds are not in your account! If this were four years ago, I would normally ignore the voice and continue to eat my breakfast but during this moment in my life I knew that God is preparing me for greatness, and I am a humbled and willing participant. I hurried to the back, opened the closest door, grabbed my purse, pulled out my phone and called the bank. Ha! All the funds were not in my account, not even half of it! In my mind, I am learning how to be patient, so I sat on the bed and said a prayer. My first words were "Lord, help me because I cannot do this on my own. Lord, I am calling upon you for guidance and strength. Lord, there are things happening around me right now that I do not understand, please help me. Lord, I know that the situation is in your hand, and I do trust you. Lord, I thank you for the power of your word and for your presence in my life in your name, Jesus, Amen. As I meditated for a minute on the word, I looked for the numbers to call to find out what was happening and no one knew anything; the loan company, the bank, or the company that paid me so what was I supposed to do, nothing but remain faithful, and that is exactly what I did. Everything in life happens for a reason. Trust me when I say I learned a lesson and that would be to be patient and keep your faith in God.

That following Sunday I did not forget to pay my tithes. Lord, I am in this to win it! Yes, Lord, use me! I have been using you for everything that I could think of prayers, strength for my father, mother, sisters, brothers, my entire family, friends, and my enemies. I will always depend and lean on you! There is no other way!

Chapter 12

As I studied the word in the Bible and focused on my lesson plans, the essays that I had to write I had enough strength to push forward. In school, I had to study Ecclesiastes, Revelation, Genesis, Exodus, and many other books which helped shape and mold me into the person that I am today, and I am so grateful.

The season was changing, and the pollen count was extremely high so most of the time when the pollen count is high, I feel terrible, I wheeze a lot. My eyes were often red and puffy. If I needed to go anywhere, I would wait until 4pm or 5pm that evening to leave the house. This day I was sitting at home watching TV and my mind begins to wonder and as I think about what I have been through. I began to praise dance and thank God for saving me. It is nothing but the Lord working on me. At that moment, I realized I cannot do anything without God and His protecting angels. In that moment, I began to call on His name and praise Him for everything that He has done for little old me, I do know that if it had not been for the Lord on my side where would I be? Lord, I thank you!

After taking the infusion treatment I went home to take a nap. This afternoon I needed some fresh air because I could not sleep. I wanted to walk around the block and think about my life. Wal-Mart was around the corner from the house, so I went there to walk and relax my nerves. As I walked around Wal-Mart, pushing a cart from one aisle to the next aisle, I began to think of the goodness of God and what He has done for me. I began to thank Him for everything because I know without Him, I would not have anything. At that moment, I was dazed out like, aww take me away, I felt free, I felt light. When I caught myself, I realized that someone was watching me. I pushed the cart to the other end of Wal-Mart on the opposite side, I looked up again after a few minutes and this young lady was watching me from afar.

I am thinking to myself if you have your purse open, close it, and pay close attention to your surroundings because someone is watching you. That is when I decided to walk around the store from one side to the other side slowly looking at the crowd and passing through the jewelry aisle, to the men department, and to the food department. It was about time for me to gather my items to leave but I had forgotten about my hair conditioner, so I went to that aisle. As I was reaching for the conditioner, I turned around to place the items in the cart my eyes connected with the young lady that was following me in Wal-Mart. We stared at each other for a minute. The way she was dressed and the way she looked caught my attention instantly. She was well dressed, and she was beautiful. I froze for a second then I reached down to put the items in my cart, suddenly, the young lady was standing near me like she did a bewitch move! We were staring into each other's eyes. The young lady began to speak by saying. I know this may seem unusual to you, but I was told to come and pray for you (at this time I am staring at her) she asked me, do you mine? I was startled!

I am sure I had this funny look on my face but anytime someone asks to pray for me I am all for it. I responded, sure I put my papers away and we were standing in the middle aisle in Wal-Mart holding hands and she began to pray. This young lady prayed for my health, strength, guidance, family, friends, and ministry.

We held hands, no one disturbed us as we were praying, and when she finished, we both said Amen. After the prayer, I continued to tell her about my journey with sarcoidosis and she stated that her mom has sarcoidosis. I reached into my purse and gave her my sarcoidosis flyer. We talked for another 5 minutes, and then she walked away. I said to myself go and tell her to make sure that her mom calls you so we can talk about how sarcoidosis has affected her.

As I walked down the aisle, I did not see her, I went down the next aisle I did not see her again. I stood there for a second and thought that was not that long ago so she could not be far. I began to jog in Wal-Mart for a second and I did not see her. I jogged throughout the store, but I did not see her. Now I am thinking to myself where did she go so fast? Now I am looking confused and puzzled, then I asked myself, what just happened? I was at the checkout, I gathered my items and, on my way, out of Wal-Mart I was still looking for her, but she was nowhere in sight.

Did I just encounter my Angel? Do you believe in Angels, I do? In *Luke 4:10*, "For it is written, He shall *give his angels charge over thee, to keep thee"* God has his way of getting our attention. When I got home, I read *Luke 22:43, "And there appeared an angel unto him from heaven, strengthening him."*

I shared my experience with my daughter, and she was amazed and so was I. Later that night, I felt a sense of calmness and peace.

Chapter 13

The next day, I woke up early feeling perfect and thanking God for this day. I cooked breakfast, cleaned the house, did the laundry, shampoo and curled my hair, cooked dinner then cleaned the dishes and vacuumed the floor because I felt awesome! That prayer did something for me. God sent His Angel to pray for little ole me and I am grateful. For the next three to four months, I felt like another person.

I have learned to be content with whatever the circumstances. I know what how it is to be in need, and I know how it is to have plenty. I have learned the secret of being content in any situation, whether well fed or hungry, whether living in plenty or in want. *"I can do all things through Christ which strengtheneth me," Philippians 4:13*. Being obedient to the word of God takes patience and prayer because it's not easy.

Because of the condition that my lungs were in from dealing with sarcoidosis, my lung specialist stated that the only option that I have right now is to have a double lung transplant. She made an appointment with the specialist at the Emory Clinic in Atlanta, Georgia.

Emory is one of the best hospitals in the world for pulmonary illnesses and it is known for personalized care for lungs and breathing disorders. Emory Hospital also has a school of medicine as well. This clinic has performed over 250-300 lung transplants with the highest survival rate in the nation.

Emory Clinic specialists offer therapies and clinical trials. This appointment included myself and my daughters. We are in the pulmonary office speaking with the physicians and weighing our options. There is so much that must be done to become a transplant recipient. We had a nice educational conversation with the doctors and was very satisfied with the doctors and their responses to our questions. We were sent home with a lot to think about and was given information to research and read. On the ride home, you could hear a pin drop. I did not say much because I felt the pain that my daughters were feeling, and it was not a good feeling. My youngest daughter did not have much to say either.

Riding alone in the car, I was talking with my God about the transplant, the rules, and the process, I would have to go through, like staying in the hospital for months and depending on my daughters who would be caring for me at least for a year and I did not want that burden on them because they are married and have families. We made it home, ate dinner and after dinner I went to my room to pray and as I kneel on my knees, I heard this smooth, calm male voice say to me, you do not need a lung transplant! I jumped up and looked around the room to make sure because I knew that I was alone, and I was. I said, okay God, I hear you! I whispered a prayer that sounded like this,

Father God, many of us need healing. I need healing for past hurts, random physical pains, depression, and health problems that I allow to ruin my days and Spiritual healing. I reach up to You to receive this healing so that I may be whole and that I may be able to then minister to others in a way that brings You fullness of glory, in your name I pray. Amen.

Despite the pain from Sarcoidosis, the biweekly doctor appointments, the major fatigue, eye pain, muscle pain, body soreness, and stiffness, I still managed to turn in my research papers, focus on college and go to church on Sundays. I felt that God had my back, and I always remembered the old saying in *I Corinthians 10:13, "No temptation has seized you except what is common to man. And God is faithful; he will not let you be tempted beyond what you can bear."* When you are tempted, he will also provide a way out so that you can stand. I have this scripture memorized for life.

I will always try my best to turn a negative situation into a positive situation. There is no room in my life for negativity. Being negative makes me feel sick to my stomach like I am a loser, and I will never accomplish anything in life. When you are negative or your thinking is negative, it has you worrying and depressed when you should not be. Going to college five days a week, I would get home, eat then I would study, do my homework, watch a little tv then pray before I went to sleep. Most of the days I would drown myself in the Bible, books, or research papers to hide or ignore my pain. I did not give myself time to think about what was really happening in my life.

My faith in God was so strong that I decided to pray about my situations and let God handle the rest. Let God decide what is the right answer for me! All I needed to do was be patient. This particular day in class a professor was talking about life and the situations that were troubling him which brought back memories for me. Later that afternoon as I sat in my room, I asked God what is it that He has planned for me? Whatever it is I will do. I will commit my life to Him. I am your child God, and you are my Father, help me, please. I spoke those words because at the time I put my trust, heart, soul, and everything I had into a man and the moment I needed him, he walked away.

I can honestly say that God picked me up out of a horrible pit, out of the *"miry clay;"* and set my feet upon a rock and established my bearings. I am forever grateful to God because if it had not been for Him by my side I do not know where I would be.

Chapter 14

My focus now is on graduating from college with my Associate Degree in Biblical Studies and to keep studying and learning about God and ways to be like Him. My days were hard and rough because I woke up tired and a lot of those mornings, I had to carry an oxygen tank with me to class every day to survive. The students, professors, and the president of the college were helpful and caring. Lord, I thank you! I attended college for two years and graduated cum laude with my Associate Degree in Biblical Studies! Lord, I thank you!

On days I would have a vision at night, I would have a dream. There were many nights I would wake up from a disturbing dream about a friend or family member and I would pray about it and go back to sleep. Some nights were worse than others. This particular night I dreamed about snakes, I was surrounded by four or five of them. I jumped up from my sleep, turned on the lights to look around my bedroom. I did not see anything, but that dream was so scary, and it felt so real! As I got out of bed, I began to pray and ask God for guidance, understanding and wisdom. I called on my prayer partner. Someone that would give me some type of feedback. I was talking with my sister, and I was telling her to watch her home because I do not know what this dream meant. People say snakes can mean death or it can mean that someone may see a snake in their home or in their yard, I am not sure. From reading my Bible and studying the word of God, I did realize that God is doing something special in my life and it is about to change drastically.

After graduating from college with my degree in Biblical Studies, I really wanted to go back and get a bachelor's degree in theology. I was seriously thinking about doing jail house ministry because there is a need for it in prison. People would tell me that I didn't need to get into that ministry because I would be exposed to a lot of people and my immune system would be compromise. Thinking about this from my point of view, I just wanted to please God; my one and only provider, friend, counselor, therapist, doctor, motivator, and lawyer.

I carried a small oxygen tank with me and if I stayed away from home, I slept on a huge oxygen tank, so I had to carry it with me everywhere I went. Carrying those two oxygen tanks around was a tiresome job but I needed them, so I did not have a choice. In the meantime, I was going home once a month and the last time I went home I ran into an old friend who has sarcoidosis. She was asking me about my oxygen tank. She wanted to know why I used it and how long have I been using it? We sat down for hours talking about sarcoidosis and from the conversation we had I decided to start a sarcoidosis support group in my hometown. I gathered information together and the next month, I planned a sarcoidosis meeting, and everything was a success. At the first meeting, we had only a few members. I have had so many people come up to me and tell me that I'm a blessing from God, and I would say to them "thank you."

In *Deuteronomy 28:2, "And all these blessings shall come on thee, and overtake thee, if thou shall hearken unto the voice of the Lord thy God."* What a blessing! From that day until this present day, we still have sarcoidosis meetings every two months in Mississippi at various locations. I am meeting different people and learning more about this mysterious disease called sarcoidosis. Everyone sees what you appear to be, very few know who you really are! Sometimes the happiest people are the ones who have been through the worst. They may be smiling but you never know what is behind those eyes. It is funny because a lot of us do that. To keep from explaining to people when someone ask me "Are you okay?" it is easier to just smile and say "Yes, I am fine." I am blessed. I do know that it is bad enough to live with an invisible illness. It is time for us to stop judging others by their appearance.

There is life after chemo treatments, there is life after two or three spinal taps for pain, there is life after infusion treatment, there is life after staying in the hospital for three to four weeks at a time, there is life after taking your insulin shots and weeks of physical therapy because of nerve damage, there is life my sarcoidosis sisters & brothers. There is life!

Chapter 15

Speaking from experiences I can say that it has been a rough and a rocky road dealing with sarcoidosis but with the grace of God I am still standing. There were many days I could not get out of bed because my joints were hurting bad, or the bottom of my feet were extremely tender and sore, so I had to creep out of bed. Many mornings I felt like I did not sleep at all because I was so tired, but I managed to push myself to start each day. When I cooked breakfast, I made sure afterward I would take my medication. Then I would sit in front of the tv for a while to rest. This happened every morning for years. I could never hold food on my stomach even after going to the doctors and taking certain medication, so odd. I was tired five days out of the week and most of the time I would move from the couch to the chair from the chair to the recliner from the recliner to the bed.

It was either pain or fatigue or both! My body had no energy and fatigue was taking over. My health was slowly changing, and I was thinking to myself what are you going to do Shelly? I knew that I did not want this for myself because I have grand babies, and I cannot play with my grands if I am tired and weak. Every morning, noon, and night I did not go to sleep before I read my Bible; the Bible was my motivator and my Savior. Reading the Bible became a habit that I did not want to break and to this day I read my Bible daily.

After breaking up from a long-term relationship, my health began to fail. I realized that the Bible was my source of strength. God has so much more that He wants me to do for Him. Reading the Bible was my breakfast, lunch, and dinner, I would not do anything until I picked up the Bible. I downloaded the Bible application on my phone to keep the Bible on hand. In *Psalms 126:5,* *"Those who sow with tears will reap with songs of joy."*

As I sat in church on Sunday, I realized that I was slipping into a depression state because of what was happening in my life. I begin to question myself, what is wrong with me? Why can't I stay in a relationship? What am I not doing? What am I doing? What do I need to do? Is it because of me or my illness? These phrases were scaring me and if you are not careful about who you talk to, or which books you read, or how strong your faith is you can sink into a deeper dark hole that you will never want to come out of called depression.

You should never forget that God loves you. God's greatest commandment is for you to love Him and to love your friend like you would your brother or sister. Thinking back a couple of months ago, it felt like I was losing everything around me, even my family. Therefore, it took some time, but I realized that I could not fully put my trust in man. The man I trust, believe, and cared for left me when I needed him the most and he did not even look back. That is when I picked up the Bible and began reading verses to help me figure out who I am. That very day is when I put my trust completely in Him. There was no other way, and I did not have another choice. Either trust and believe in God or sink into that dark place. Depression can leave you feeling emotionless.

I am the type of person that believes if you really want something bad enough you will make a way to get it. To every problem, there is a solution, and I am willing to push myself until I find a solution. Nothing takes God by surprise. The same God that holds the universe up with one hand, takes hold of me by my right hand. And *Psalms 46:10* says, *"Be still and know that I am God."*

At the age of forty-one, my life was headed in the wrong direction, and I knew that I needed to make some choices in life because I have four grandbabies who I love dearly. Following Christ is the best decision I have ever made! In *Romans 5:8*, it states *"But God commendeth his love towards us, in that, while we were yet sinners, Christ died for us."*

I graduated from Bible College Cum Laude with a 4.0 GPA. The Lord knew that I struggled to finish college, but He also knew that I was determined. As I sit here thinking about my life and the obstacles that I had faced I realized that I had a dream and quitting was not an option for me. Attending classes, writing essays & papers, taking tests, and reading the Bible every day saved my life. As I attended classes, my body was getting tired. Keep in mind every day I was carrying an oxygen tank to school; I could not go anywhere without them. Those tanks were very heavy, but I did not have a choice. The doctor stated that I needed to carry one every day to save my life. God has brought me an exceptionally long way. I am acting as if the things that happen were controlled by man, it is not so. It is interesting how disobedience can not only delay the will of God in your life, but it can completely cancel the plan of God for our life.

The more I tried to ignore the fact that God was molding me the worse my life situations were getting. I would run if I could. My mind is always occupied with the thought of the Lord using me. Silently, I would pray. Reading the Bible or anything that pertains to God was my focus. I began fasting, reading the Bible more, going to Sunday school and Wednesday night Bible study weekly.

Undeniable Faith

Chapter 16

I asked God to continue to write the story of my life because He knows my purpose in life and He knows how He wants me to live my life. God has called me by my name, and I have answered! From studying the word of God, I have learned to be more patient, observant, and obedient to others especially my mom and dad, my Queen, and my King. We should always keep this passage in mine. In *Ephesians 6:1, "Children, obey your parents in the Lord: for this is right."* Being a fool will get you nowhere.

I began to have those dreams and visions of family members and friends in despair or in trouble. The more I prayed to God the closer I felt His love, guidance, and peace in my life. Life gets rough sometimes and you need someone to talk to and if you do not have that person, family member or friend to go to then what? What do you do? Talk to the man above, God!

My father and I talk to each other at least three times a week. When I was younger, my dad was not around at all to see me grow up. We really did not know where he was or whether he was dead or alive. At an early age, we moved from Chicago to a small town in the South and left my dad behind. We did not stay connected at all, but I always knew when I was able, I would reach out to him. Many years had passed, and I was undecided about reaching out to him. In 35 years, we have never heard another word from him. It took about eight months, but we finally were able to see one another again. I had to find his sister who lived in Chicago, and she helped me to contact my dad. From that day to this day, we stay in contact with one another, and we visit each other as often as we can.

My dad and mom are the reasons that I am here today, and I do not take that lightly. My parents are my priority. My siblings and I are close and because I have sarcoidosis, we stay in contact with each other because we never know when I may have a flare up which most of the time sends me to the hospital. My younger brother who lived in Texas has been having stomach pain and we would talk about how the pain bothers him a lot, but he does not like to take medication for the pain.

This particular morning, I was fasting and praying to God asking Him for forgiveness and clarity on life. I will never forget the Holy Spirit touched my soul and I was moved to talk to my brother about the symptoms and problems he was having with his stomach. I held on to that thought for two weeks because I did not want to talk to Daniel about it. I did not have a choice. Why did I say that I did not have a choice? Because the Holy Spirit was picking at me. I was crushed but I also was concerned. It took me two weeks, but I sat my brother down and suggested that he go to the doctor to find a solution to his stomach issues. He stated that he would go but months passed.

One day Daniel was weak, feeling sick to his stomach so he decided he needed to make a doctor's appointment. The appointment date came. Daniel went to his appointment, and he needed blood work and more tests done. That same week my dad called to let me know that he was going to the doctor because he did not feel well, and he wanted to make sure his blood count was normal. My dad had sarcoidosis in his eyes many years ago and his right eye was damaged by sarcoidosis and the doctors had to replace his right eye with a marble eye. The left eye went into remission five years ago and the sarcoidosis has not come back. My dad only had sarcoidosis in his eyes and no other organs were affected. He no longer has any problems with sarcoidosis. As of today, my dad is in remission. God has healed my dad and He can heal me too all I need to do is to be patient and have faith in God's work and in His timing.

The following week my brother came home from Texas, and he wanted to talk with the family. We gathered to talk about the results of his test. The test results came back that he has colon cancer, and he needs to start treatments. Everyone was quiet for a while then I began to say trust God and let us do this! He will not let you down! This was a test result that I did not want to hear but God always has the last say in everything that we do. We also need to keep in mind that we are only here on earth temporarily. This place is not our permanent home!

The next day, which was Monday, my dad had a doctor's appointment. After his appointment, he called me to say that his text results had come back and that he has colon cancer. Lord, I could have fainted, but I thought about my dad! A seventy-five-year-old man has colon cancer, and he must take 60-day treatments of chemo and radiation. My God be a fence for us, please! My dad had to start radiation and chemo treatment 5 days a week for two months. So, I am thinking to myself is this a dream or what? I began to think to myself you cannot get weak or break down because you know your dad calls you all the time and you do not want him to hear the pain in your voice. My brother lives in Texas so every chance that I can get we would drive to Texas; me, his sons, and our mom. We would stay for two or three weeks at a time. I needed to focus on God and remain faithful and prayerful for the two most important men in my life because they were dealing with cancer and taking treatments.

Undeniable Faith

Chapter 17

Being the oldest of five, I tried my best to love and care for my sibling. To me, family means the world to me. That is why every chance that I could visit my brother in Texas I would visit. It means a lot when family can support you and be by your side when you need them the most. There are so many verses in the Bible that I can relate to and I always find myself quoting *Matthew 17:20, "And Jesus said unto them, Because of your unbelief: for verily I say unto you, If ye have faith as a grain of mustard seed, ye shall say unto this mountain, Remove hence to yonder place; and it shall remove; and nothing shall be impossible unto you".*

There have been days where I felt alone, days when I just didn't want to get out of bed. Getting out of bed was not an option I needed to do that for me. Everyday has been a challenge but by the grace of God I pushed even harder. My dad had 30 days of radiation and chemo treatments. On the weekend, he would get rest because he was very tired from the treatment. My mom wanted to visit my brother and I knew that she would not go if I did not go with her. We decided to visit and spend some time with my brother while he was taking treatments. He started out with his doctor appointments, and everything was going well until he had to go to an appointment every week. He was the type of person that never got sick, or he never went to the doctor for anything. As the season changed, his sinuses started acting up and he would get over the counter medication, but he never had to go to a doctor to sit in the waiting room or to have a test done until now. Right before he started his treatments, he began to have stomach pains which hurt so bad he would have to take something for the pain.

I knew he was in pain because he had to take something for the pain. He did not like to take medication. One day, we were on our way to an appointment, and he was having pain and he did not want to take the pain medicine. He fell to the floor and as I stood over him, I whispered to him, "you can do this God's got you and I will not leave your side." He slowly raised up then he stood up. From listening to him describe the pain he was feeling and seeing him in pain the journey was extremely hard. The medication he was taking on a regular basis for chemo and the aftereffects often left him very weak.

Prayer is my weapon and I use it every day. What is prayer? Prayer is communicating with the higher power for the purpose of thanksgiving or a praise report. Prayer is an important part of my life now because I believe that it can keep your life in balance, and it helps with my peace of mind and guidance. My best prayer when I am walking, driving, or sitting down, I will pray anywhere as long as He can hear me, I am sanctified. Now I know why people say cancer sucks! In *Romans 8:31, "What shall we then say to these things? If God be for us, who can be against us?"*

Those were the days that I laid in bed and whispered a prayer in which it sounded something like this; God help me so I can help my brother and be there for my father. I can't do this by myself. I have tried and failed. I need you to carry me. I need someone to lean on Lord. Strengthen my brother and my father and please help them to rise and be healed like only you can Lord. Help me to lift my worry and burdens to you, Lord. You are our strength. In your name Lord I pray. Amen.

My faith in God was through the roof. I had no one and nothing to lean on but God and that is exactly what I did. I was praying for my dad and my brother to be healed from prostate and colon cancer. My feelings were all over the place, I did not want to stress or worry too much because I did not want to have a sarcoidosis flare up. Every day for two months, I needed extra strength to keep going. I was not ready for half of the mess that I went through but with the grace of God I made it through!

By the grace of God, my dad went through chemo and radiation treatments for two months 5 days a week and he is now doing perfectly fine. God saw fit to let him live longer to enjoy his family and to serve Him. I truly thank God for these blessings, and I owe the Lord my life. In the month of May, my dad got his health report. The cancer was gone, and he was doing fine. He no longer needed to take radiation or chemo treatments. What a blessing! I have said to myself many days and nights, Lord have mercy on me, I can't do this without you.

In the meantime, my brother was still dealing with the strong medication, sleepless nights, pain, dry mouth, mind, and heart racing and so many other emotions. Being the oldest, I knew that he has never dealt with so much pain, I mean no more than a headache from being too hungry but nothing like this. This was one test he was not going to go through alone. As days and weeks passed from the month of February, March, and April, Daniel went through a series of tests, hospital stays and medication. I knew it was hard on him so I tried my best to stay by his side, to call and check on him whenever I could. The doctor thinks that in our family cancer is inherited, which is why I mention getting tested to my siblings and nephews often.

Early detection and warning signs can help prevent surgery and more. One or two early signs of cancer may be constipation, diarrhea, or your stools may start to change in color or shape. Those were not Daniel signs; he went to the doctor and was prescribed medication for hemorrhoids. The medication was taken for three to four months, and he had to go to the doctor again, this time the test results came back; cancer. A lot of people say the big "C" word. When some people hear the word cancer, their heart skips a beat, they begin to cry, or you just take a deep breathe. It is like your entire world has stops!

Chapter 18

Paying attention to your body and what you eat are important parts of being healthy. My mom and I would travel to Texas to spend time with Daniel and to be by his side. I know from experience that needles, taking blood, and different tests all the time can be draining. I knew that he would need someone to cheer him on or just to be there for support. This particular day he had a test done because he was having muscle spasm in his stomach. He was lying in the hospital bed. I said, "Just try to take the pain." He said, "Shoot! Not this pain!" I said, "I have muscle spasm in my chest." I said that to see if it would help to calm him down a bit, no it did not!

He said sister I do not see how you do this; you are a strong woman stronger than me. I said you can do it; I am here, and we are going to do this together. People say that I am that type of sister, aunt, cousin if I can help you in any way, I will. I feel like family should come together when there is sickness and death. Quality time is important. Therefore, I have realized that just because he or she does not support you, I will. And it does not matter who you are if you need me, I will be there if I can. I thank God for my dad. He is doing better and is in remission from prostate cancer so now I can focus on being there for my brother.

When Daniel was home, he spent time talking to the men in his family and his men friends. He let them know what was going on with him. He also said to them how scared he was but at that time being scared pushed him into a corner. He informed the guys about going to the doctor for testing for polyps. When I saw him doing that, I was so happy and proud of my brother because the guys needed to hear that kind of information coming from someone who has been through it. There have been days where I thanked God for blessing us, myself, and my brother of 50 years to be able to come together and love on one another.

A couple of weeks passed and three of the guys that my brother had spoken with earlier about his situation went to the doctor. The doctor found polyps and they were happy that they spoke with Daniel, and I was ecstatic as well. God works in mysterious ways meaning his ways are not ours and his thoughts are not our thoughts! If you, do it God's way, I am sure it would be something completely opposite.

In *Isaiah 55:8-9*; *"For my thoughts are not your thoughts, neither are your ways my ways, saith the Lord. For as the heavens are higher than the earth, so are my ways higher than your ways and my thoughts than your thoughts."* Here is another one that I love! In *Jeremiah 29:11; "For I know the thoughts that I think toward you, said the Lord, thoughts of peace, and not of evil, to give you an expected end."* This battle was a tough, rough, and painful one, still I did not leave his side. When I could be there, we were there. When we had to leave Texas to travel to Mississippi, we assured Daniel to fight and pray, he said that is all I do. I knew right then his faith in God was there and that is all he needed. I needed to know that he was depending on the Lord! My brother assured me that he has accepted that God is using him and this test he intends on passing. My thoughts were, thank you God!

For some people putting your trust in something that you have never seen before is crazy and hard but to some it is hard but doable. In *James 1:2-4*; *"My brethren, count it all joy when ye fall into divers temptation; knowing this, that the trying of your faith worketh patience. But let patience have her perfect work, that ye may be perfect and entire, wanting nothing."* My God, I love you with all my heart for without you there would be no me. Without you Lord I believe that I would be some place locked up because you have helped me change my life and I am forever grateful.

Days and months passed, and Daniel was not getting much relief from pain, and he was taking pain medication often. I was bothered a bit because he was taking pain medication. If you're not careful, you can get addicted to the medication, and we did not need that. I will never forget the names of these drugs; Percocet, Fentanyl and Morphine or how they made him feel. Lord, thank you for watching over Daniel, my dad, myself, and the rest of my family. I could not have done this without you, I love you Lord forever, Amen. Daniel began to have issues with painful urination and itchy rashes around his waist. We made an appointment to see the doctor. The appointment was a week later. In the meantime, the doctor suggested that we use a cream for the itching. This is something different and it made him so uncomfortable. It hurt me to my heart but remained a faithful and loving sister to stay by his side. I asked to see where he was itching around his waist. He removed the covers, and on his stomach, there were large bumps. This itching was something new. The week passed and the itching around his waist was getting worse. We went to the doctor's appointment; tests were done, blood work was taken, and he had to stay overnight at the hospital because of his excruciating pain and the terrible itching. We could not stay overnight with him because of Covid so we went home.

The corona virus is a family of viruses that can cause illnesses such as the cold and severe acute respiratory syndrome. What a disaster that a lot of people have lost family members and friends because of this virus. In *Philippians 4:13*, it states *"I can do all things through Christ which strengtheneth me."* I had to constantly repeat this scripture every day. I needed strength to help Daniel.

The next day, we patiently waited for the doctor to

come and discuss the results of Daniel's tests. When they did, I was shocked, and I honestly felt helpless and lightheaded. The doctors stated that the cancer had rapidly spread to his bladder. It's a rare form of cancer that they do not see often and because he was so weak, he couldn't take the chemo or the radiation. The doctors also stated that they could not do anything else to help relieve his pain or help with that rare form of bladder cancer.

Chapter 19

My heart skipped a beat. My eyes rolled to the back of my head. The Lord knows that I felt weak and confused but then something said, "Shelly, snap out of it!" Daniel must be told so you need to get a grip. That moment will forever resonate in my mind, forever. After sitting down and explaining to him what was going on, his faith in God was so strong, he said, I do not believe them so let us get a second opinion? He did not know that this opinion was a third opinion! Jesus! Jesus! I had to ease his mind somehow, so I said, okay if that is what you want then that is what we are going to do! This is a feeling that I have never felt before in my life. As we prepared to take him home to be on hospice, I continued to ask the Lord for strength because I was getting weak. I had no other choice but to quote scriptures and pray, pray, and pray.

In *2 Samuel 22:23*; *"God is my strength and power : and he maketh my way perfect"*. My friend, comforter, way-maker, I need you! Lord, I am asking you to come see about my family and I so we can care for my brother. During that devastating news, I called my dad to see how he was doing. He was done with chemo and radiation, but some days were better than others. The hospital brought him home and before I entered his room, I mumbled a prayer because I needed it. Our mom, niece, sisters, sons, cousins, and brother shared many moments with him. God knew exactly what he needed, and it was done. Family was together at that moment to comfort and to love on him. We rubbed his feet, his bald head, and massage his legs everything he asked for was given to him. I could feel the pain from the family, but God's will shall be done.

When I woke up that morning, I had several missed calls and texts about a family friend. My brother had been admitted into the hospital. My faith and my belief in God are the only things that kept me going because right now I am running low on everything else. My thought process right now, this dream I had last night, the friend that I am talking about is someone I had grew up with. So right now, I am like Lord whatever it is you are doing in this season please do not do it without me!

In *Hebrews 11:1*; *"Now faith is substance of things hoped for, the evidence of things not seen."*

This day I was a mess, and this is the reason! The dream that I had was about two people that were extremely ill and had to be admitted into the hospital for care. They both stayed in the hospital on a ventilator for weeks. I can remember that one of the people in my dream got better and went home to be in hospice and the other person passed away. Jesus! Jesus! What I am not saying guys is that one of the people that was in my dream was my brother, Daniel! This dream I tried to ignore but I could not, and it was weighing heavy on my heart. I kept calling on the Lord, asking to come to see about Daniel and Hector. As each day passed, I would call and check on Daniel and Hector. Keep in mind that every time that I have those dreams in two to three weeks something happens. After that third week, we got that phone call to come to Texas because Daniel was not doing well. My trust and faith were in God, I had no choice but to put on that full armor of God. I whispered to God we are leaning on you and your mighty power.

  The immediate family travelled from Mississippi, Minnesota, and Georgia to be by Daniel's side. He was surrounded by love. His loving wife of 10 years did her part and for that reason the family is forever grateful! As we cared for him, loved on him, and comforted him, we knew his days were passing. He was in less pain, less medicine we had to give him. As I stood by his bedside, I prayed to the Lord to ease the pain and to comfort my brother doing this critical time. I ask the Lord to be with my family because we do not know what to do or what to say to each other right now. There was someone by his side every minute he was never left alone.

I decided to talk with him. He could not say anything but move his finger or arm. After the conversation with him, I played his favorite song by Rance Allen (Rest His Soul) and he began to move a finger, what a feeling! The family was by his side until we could not be by his side. As I stood by his bedside and held his hand, I made a promise to him, and I will keep it until I can't! God knew my brother was tired. Everyone can't endure pain. Death is a part of life, and it is something that we will never get used to. I thank God for the 50 years we shared with Daniel and for the good ole days and the bad days. In June 2020, was his last day on earth and I was holding his hand.

By the grace of God, I am still standing, and I will forever be grateful and humble. My brother, and friend, we miss you, but we know that you are in a better place watching over us. I feel some comfort knowing that you are watching over us, (Our Angel). Throughout the trials and tribulations, I have experienced, I have patience and love to share with others. I am ready to show the world that God will make a way. The only thing that you need to do is to have that tiny bit of faith. Just a little bit of faith will take you a long way. He did it for me and he will do it for you. In *Psalms 34:1*, it states, *"I will bless the Lord at all times: his praise shall continually be in my mouth."*

The trials and tribulations that we experienced in life will lead you closer to God. For twenty years, I have been walking by faith and not by sight. Faith has brought me a long way and I have God to thank for it. The Bible will forever be a book that I will cherish for the rest of my life. In *Ephesians 2:8*; *"For by grace are ye saved through faith ; and that not of yourselves: it is the gift of God.* From being used and abused by men, relationships and family members and thinking that you did not have anywhere to turn too, I turn to God and ask Him to use me so I can be more like Him. I have learned from experience that man will let you down but if you put your trust in the Lord you will win every time. I've been struggling with a mysterious disease for over 25 years to dealing with devastating cancer diagnosis from my dad to my brother then death. Serving the Lord with all my heart is all that I need. Keep in mind, God knows.

In *Romans 8:28*, it states, *"and we know that all things work together for good to them that love God, to those who are called according to his purpose."* In *Romans 12:2*; *"And be not conformed to this world: but be ye transformed by the renewing of your mind, that ye may prove what is that good, and acceptable, and perfect, will of God.* Life can be rough, tough, depressing and so much more, but I think that life is what you make of it. The Lord has been using me and guiding me for so long I refuse to go back the other way. Giving God the praises and showing Him how much I love Him and how much I would love to be like Him and sharing the love with my fellow sisters and brothers.

Chapter 20

As I reflected over the last couple of months about how our lives have changed dramatically since my younger brother's passing from cancer. I remember the dreams and the visions I saw but I tried so hard to ignore them. I knew the Lord was using me! I knew the Lord was preparing me for something much bigger than I could imagine but I tried to ignore it. There have been many nights I dreamed of family or friends in car accidents which scared me to the core. I would get on my knees and pray. There have been many nights I dreamed of a friend pregnant and losing a baby because of being disobedient. I would wake up crying. Then get on my knees to pray.

The Lord revealed husbands cheating on their wives because they can, the wives knew this but refused to acknowledge the facts because they loved their husbands. I would get out of bed and pray for people that I did not know, and I would get out of bed and pray for people that I knew. I know how God has wired me in two to three weeks this vision or dream will become real. God has been sending me signs and I have been having dreams and visions for years, but this dream I did want to think twice about. This night I watched my favorite show, Chicago police officers and I prepared myself for bed around 11 o'clock pm.

Around 4 am, I woke up crying hysterically for about 30 minutes; my nose running, and my eyes blood shot red. I got out of bed, wiped my eyes and nose, got on my knees, and prayed like I have never prayed before in my life. This dream had me nervous and scared and I knew that I would need strength to endure the pain, and nervousness. I knew my family members and friends would need strength. This prayer was for strength for everyone! The prayer:

Lord, please give us strength it is in your hands Lord, we need you now. Lord, give us wisdom to understand whatever we may be facing and thank you Lord for being here for us. Whatever it is Lord we cannot do anything without you. Lord, you are our light, and we need you to guide us, please in your name Lord. Amen!

From that day forward, I had to stand firm because I was going to be in his presence, and I refused to let him see me break. My belt buckle was tight around my waist, breast plate ready and as I was being fitted, I put on the helmet of salvation and was carrying the sword of the spirit, the word of God! I was prepared! Lord, I thank you for your grace and mercy for without it I would not be here. Lord, I am grateful through all the issues with molestation from family members, glaucoma, depression, nerve problems, migraine headaches, anxiety, diabetes, body aches, heart disease and respiratory problems. Still, you loved me enough to wake me up to care for my family and elderly friends. For this, I will forever give you praise!

At some point in life, you will have to let go. It does not matter what you do or how you do it, some things are just not meant to be. Everybody will go through trials and tribulations, and it is up to you to figure out how you come out of it. You can either learn a lesson or experience a blessing it is on you. I love the Lord and He heard my cry, and I am forever his vessel that wants to be used by Him.

To this day I am God's masterpiece, and He is my healer, counselor, provider, therapist, best friend, doctor, supplier, and my way maker, who is who you are. In *Ephesians 2:10*, *"For we are His workmanship, created in Christ Jesus for good works, which God hath before ordained that we should walk in them."*

Think of a masterpiece:
a jewel, a prize,
or a show piece!
Special right?
Trust Him!

About The Author

Shelly Clanton is a dedicated Sarcoidosis Advocate who is committed to bringing awareness to a debilitating and devastating disease. She graduated Cum Laude from Carver Bible College in Atlanta, Georgia with an Associate of Arts Degree in Biblical Studies.

While working tirelessly and consistently, the House of Representative for the State of Mississippi presented me with the proclamation for Sarcoidosis. With this proclamation, the state of Mississippi will recognize the month of April as Sarcoidosis Month. Shelly is working on several projects now including her second book, "**Undeniable Faith, How God Kept Me.**"

She currently resides in Mississippi. She enjoys cooking, spending quality time with her grands, her family, and helping the elderly in her neighborhood. I hope you are blessed with this project!